BRIGHT IDEAS FOR
Busy Moms

7 Positive Strategies for Raising Great Kids

KAROL LADD

THOMAS NELSON
Since 1798

NASHVILLE   DALLAS   MEXICO CITY   RIO DE JANEIRO   BEIJING

Bright Ideas for Busy Moms
Copyright © 2007 by Karol Ladd

Published in Nashville, Tennessee, by Thomas Nelson, Inc.

Unless otherwise indicated, Scripture quotations are taken from:
Holy Bible, the New Living Translation © 1996. Used by permission of Tyndale House Publishers, Inc., Wheaton, Illinois. All rights reserved.

Other Scripture quotations are taken from:
The Holy Bible, New International Version of the Bible (NIV) © 1984 by the International Bible Society. Used by permission of Zondervan Bible Publishers; *New American Standard Bible* (NASB) © 1960, 1962, 1963, 1971, 1972, 1973, 1975, and 1977 by the Lockman Foundation, and are used by permission; and *The Holy Bible*, New King James Version (NKJV) ©1979, 1980, 1982, 1992, Thomas Nelson, Inc. Used by permission.

Project Editor: Lisa Stilwell

Designed by Susan Browne Design, Nashville, Tennessee

ISBN 10: 1–4041–0428–3
ISBN 13: 978–1–4041–0428–0

Printed and bound in China

www.thomasnelson.com

CONTENTS

Introduction: Simply Smart Parenting 1

POSITIVE STRATEGY #1

Bring Out the Best in Your Kids

Discovering Your Kids' Strengths 6

Creative Ways to Encourage 10

Accentuate the Positive; Eliminate the Negative. 14

POSITIVE STRATEGY #2

Discipline with Wisdom, Discernment, and Love

Fresh Ideas for Effectively Changing Your Kids' Behavior . . . 20

How to Train Your Kids from the Inside Out 24

Three Essentials for the Mom at Her Wit's End 28

POSITIVE STRATEGY #3

Open Up the Lines of Communication

What to Say when They Won't Listen 34

How to Listen when They Won't Talk 38

Strengthen Your Kids' Conversational Skills 44

POSITIVE STRATEGY #4

Teach Character Qualities and Moral Values

Teachable Moments Make a Difference 52

Books, Movies, Music, and More Can Be Tools 57

Teach Your Kids to Be Good Citizens. 63

POSITIVE STRATEGY #5

Help Your Kids Develop an Intimacy with God

Encouraging a Love for God's Word. 70

Four Basic Truths about Prayer Every Child Needs to Learn. . 74

Fun Ideas for Scripture Memory 80

POSITIVE STRATEGY #6

Be a Positive Role Model

No One Is Perfect 90

Qualities Your Kids Need to See in You. 94

Goals, Not Regrets 100

POSITIVE STRATEGY #7

Prepare Your Kids for Life

Increasing Their Social IQ 106

What Every Child Should Know Before Leaving Home . . . 109

Working Hard or Hardly Working? 113

Concluding Thoughts 118

Before I got married, I had six theories about bringing up children; now I have six children and no theories.

— Lord Rochester

INTRODUCTION

Simply Smart Parenting

Let's lay it all out on the table. This job of motherhood is a little tougher than we thought it would be. Do you agree? Our life is no longer our own, we are stretched in a million different directions, and sometimes we have to admit that we don't exactly know what we're doing. Motherhood began with changing diapers and feeding babies, and it quickly grew into driving the car pool, helping with homework, refereeing sibling disagreements, getting kids to practice, and dealing with feelings that have been hurt by the birthday-party invitation that didn't come or the thoughtless words of classmates and even friends. I'm guessing you may feel slightly overwhelmed at times. I know I do. Yet despite the tug we feel in so many different directions, our deep-down desire is to focus on loving our kids and raising them to love God and have a positive impact on this world.

This goal is clear, but sometimes it seems so hard to reach because the minutiae of life get in the way. Although it would be nice to sit down and read several lengthy books providing in-depth strategies on successful parenting, the reality is if you actually did have time to read a lengthy instructional book, you'd sit down and fall asleep within minutes. What you really need is an informative, to-the-point book with a simple and straightforward format that works with your busy schedule. Congratulations! You've found it. You can read this book in the car-pool line, while you are waiting for an appointment, or over a cup of coffee with a friend. You can even study it with other moms in your neighborhood; it can serve as a catalyst for getting to know one another. The chapters are short, and the principles are doable for moms with kids of any age.

My desire is to encourage and inspire you as well as provide you with the nuts and bolts of positive and wise parenting. The good news is that smart parenting doesn't come from filling our minds with an overload of information; rather, it comes from applying a few wise strategies and doing so with a heart filled with love. May this book touch your heart and direct your thoughts in a way that will have a lasting and positive impact on your family. More importantly, may you be reminded throughout the pages in this book that you are not alone in this parenting journey. You have a wonderful heavenly Father who loves you and is with you each step of the way.

POSITIVE

God has given each of us
the ability to do certain
things well.

ROMANS 12:6

STRATEGY ONE

BRING OUT THE BEST IN YOUR KIDS

It's our job as parents to help our kids discover their strengths and gifts and see their potential.

Discovering Your Kids' Strengths

Craig Randall drove a garbage truck for a living in his hometown of Peabody, Massachusetts. One day as he was getting ready to empty a trash container, he noticed a Wendy's soft-drink cup with a contest sticker still attached. The week before he had won a chicken sandwich when he pulled a sticker off a cup, so he was hoping to win some fries or a soft drink this time. Much to Craig's surprise, he peeled the sticker and found it was worth $200,000—money he could use toward the construction of a new home![1]

A careless person discarded the cup as trash, but Craig saw its potential and found a great treasure in the process. We may not always find the winning sticker in a contest, but we will always be a winner when we are looking for the treasure in people, especially the treasure in our kids. Every person is created with unique gifts, talents, and abilities that are just waiting to be discovered. When we look for the treasure in people, we will never come up empty-handed. The key is that we must be *looking* for the sparkling gems and shiny gold nuggets in others. As moms, we have the opportunity to look for the treasure within each of our kids, help them discover their one-of-a-kind gifts and talents, and then provide them opportunities to sharpen those abilities.

God has given every child unique gifts and talents, and we have the privilege of uncovering and developing them in our kids. Consider the story told of a sculptor named Antonio who chipped away at a huge piece of stone, but eventually decided he couldn't do anything with it. He pushed the stone aside so he could work on another project. Later, Michelangelo carved from that stone one of the greatest works of all times: the statue of David. Michelangelo was able to see the potential that Antonio didn't.

How do we discover the potential in our kids? Simply by observing them. Plain and simple, as we study their natural bents, we begin to see glimmers of possibilities. The challenge we moms face so often, though, is to not be so focused on what our kids are doing wrong that we miss what they can do right. Certainly, we should be on the lookout for times when we must discipline and train our kids, but we also need to be looking for their potential and their gifts.

Here are three tools to help you on your treasure hunt:

1. **Seek God's Help:** As we pray for each of our kids individually, we can ask God to open our eyes to the gifts He has given them.

2. **Spend Time Together:** Never underestimate the power of a little one-on-one time with each of your children. This is an opportunity to hear their unique voice, understand their interests, and begin to see their desires and sense the direction their talents and interests might take them.

3. **Seize Opportunities:** Discover ways you can help your kids pursue their interests and develop their talents. As you look for opportunities for your children—ranging from classes to contests to competitions—these experiences not only enhance their skills but also show them that you believe in them and their abilities.

Keep in mind that each one of your children is a precious and unique creation. You can't expect each child in your family to display the same abilities and talents as the other kids in the family. So work to identify each child's unique bent and then build on it. Often we fall into the trap of wanting all our kids to take piano or play soccer. Sometimes we think that if all the other first-grade parents are putting their kids in gymnastics, we need to do the same. You may put your child in for a short class to see if she has an interest or an aptitude, but steer away from overwhelming both your child and yourself with activities or sports just because "everyone else is doing it."

So look for the treasure in each of your children. Not one of them is exactly like you or your husband, and not one of them is exactly like any of their siblings. Each child is a beautiful creation and a treasure chest of abilities, gifts, and talents. Again, build on their unique bent. If they love to draw and create, encourage their artistic side. If they walk around the house singing and dancing, explore their performing-arts ability. If they are running around outside, kicking or throwing a ball, build on that. If they love animals, develop their interest. The key to having great expectations for our kids is realizing it's not all about *our* great plans for our children, but about *God's* great plans and purpose for them—plans that will enable them to use the unique gifts and talents He has given them.

Creative Ways to Encourage

The word *encourage* means "to give strength." The root *cor* comes from the Latin word meaning "heart." We strengthen our kids' hearts through the encouraging messages we offer. Most of us have not had the benefit of a Parenting 101 class to teach us how to encourage our kids. Some people actually lived in a positive home environment where they saw their parents model encouragement. Most people, however, didn't have that kind of example in their growing-up years. Whatever our past experience, we can all learn and develop creative ways to bring a new and fresh spirit into our home with our uplifting words.

Our kids' best qualities grow and grow when they are fed the delicious morsels of kind and encouraging words. What qualities do you want to see in your kids? Be on the lookout for those qualities and, when you see them lived out, seize the opportunity to encourage your kids with a good word. Our kids live up to our expectations, good or bad. So let's make sure we are giving our kids positive accolades and attention for what they are doing right. That starts with being on the lookout for those good qualities.

Johann von Goethe said, "Treat a man as he appears to be, and you make him worse. But treat a man as if he already were what he potentially could be, and you make him what he should be."[2] Apparently Goethe's very own mother was a perfect example of this positive outlook. Read what was said of her:

> She had such a sunny, unselfish nature, that she was always happy herself, and always tried to make others happy. Her eyes only looked for all that was best in other people, and fault-finding was unknown to her.[3]

Don't we all want to be like Goethe's dear mother, seeing only the good in others? It's too easy to focus on what our kids are doing wrong. But as we do our motherly duty of searching for what they are doing wrong, we sometimes forget to look for what they are doing right, even if those right things are pretty basic. For instance, when was the last time you scolded your children in the checkout line at the grocery store because they were whining and complaining? Do you think to say anything on those occasions (rare as they may be) when your kids are good in the checkout line?

Let's determine to be like searchlights as we hunt down those stellar moments and then affirm our kids for them: "Honey, you were so kind to the woman at the library today. I really appreciate it"; or "Sweetheart, I noticed your patience while we waited for your sister at the doctor's office. Good job." You'll see your kids smile and sit up a little taller when their good qualities have been noted.

When you encourage your kids, you need to:

- **Be Sincere.** Flattery will get you nowhere. Your kids recognize unfounded praise a mile away, and such empty words will cause you to lose credibility with them. Offer only honest and realistic words of encouragement based on truth. Find truthful and good things to say *about* your children *to* your children.

- **Be Direct.** Tell your kids exactly what you like about them and be specific. Don't stop with "Great job!" Go on to say, "Great job at your recital / in your game / helping out at home today.

I was impressed by the way you persevered/ concentrated/_____."

🐝 **Be Creative.** Your praise and words of encouragement don't need to be verbal. Consider writing a note or sending a text message or e-mail. One mom I know uses dry-erase markers to write notes on the kids' bathroom mirror.

Although we wish we were naturally positive people continually overflowing with uplifting words, the truth is that the cares of motherhood and the details of life sometimes distract us from our nobler goals. I find that it helps to have little reminders around the house to stimulate my thinking about what my kids are doing right.

You might find it helpful, for instance, to write yourself little notes and put them in the laundry room or by the kitchen sink. Those reminders could be as simple as writing the word *Encourage* on a sticky note.

I use the image of the Eiffel Tower to

remind myself to encourage my kids. I know that sounds strange, but many years ago our family had the rare opportunity to take a trip to Paris with my husband's company. I prepared my daughters for the adventure by telling them all about the monuments and sights we would see. Perhaps I went a little overboard on the Eiffel Tower issue, because everywhere we went in Paris (from the moment our plane touched down to the time we left), they were looking for the Eiffel Tower. And they found it every time! Why? Because they were looking for it! What are the Eiffel Towers in your kid's life, the good qualities you want to nurture and encourage? If you're looking for them, you'll find them.

Accentuate the Positive; Eliminate the Negative

In 1940, Johnny Mercer wrote the lyrics for a catchy song called "Accentuate the Positive." Not a bad theme song for us moms, wouldn't you agree? After all, it is our job—

among many others!—to draw attention to the positive attributes in our kids, to notice and acknowledge their good deeds, kind words, and selfless actions. The flip side of our job is—again in the words of the song—to "eliminate the negative." We do this through wise and thoughtful discipline, a parenting strategy we'll discuss in the next section. Right now we'll focus on accentuating the positive.

Never underestimate the effect of your words of affirmation and appreciation on your kids. And remember those accolades can come in all shapes and sizes. You can offer your kids encouragement with a hug or a smile or by simply being there. The bottom line in parenting is that our kids need our time and attention when they are doing something right. All too often kids get their parents' attention only when they are doing something wrong. (This tendency calls for a different song: "Accentuate the Negative"!) As parents we must make an intentional effort to pay attention to the positive, not the negative.

When it comes to emphasizing the good, we parents can choose from a multitude of possibilities. Certainly, as we talked about earlier, our encouraging words give a big boost to our kids, but there are other ways to show them our support. Consider the following options:

- ❧ Volunteer as a leader or helper for their favorite activity.
- ❧ Search for local exhibits or shows that appeal to their interests or talents and then go together.
- ❧ Attend their performances and athletic events.
- ❧ Invite their friends over and get to know them.
- ❧ Fix their favorite dinner or snack.
- ❧ Make a special plate or banner to celebrate special achievements or occasions.
- ❧ Give a flower or small gift with a note of appreciation.
- ❧ Visit your kids at school for lunch or take them out.
- ❧ Go on a short trip or a day trip—just the two of you.
- ❧ Play a game or do an art project of their choice.
- ❧ Occasionally help them do their chores.
- ❧ Go for a walk together and tell them how special they are to you.

Remember, simple things such as a listening ear, eye contact when you're talking together, and a warm smile can be just the encouragement our kids need to move forward with confidence. Our ultimate goal is to build up what is good in our children, and we do this by affirming them for what they are doing right. Just as an accent mark tells us which syllable to emphasize in a word, our accent marks of attention show our kids what we are emphasizing. So let's be diligent in emphasizing the strengths of each of our kids. When we are, we'll see some of the negatives dissipate in the process. ❧

You never know when a moment and a few sincere words can have an impact on a life.

—

Zig Ziglar

POSITIVE

2

Train a child in the way he should go, and when he is old he will not turn from it.

PROVERBS 22:6 NIV

STRATEGY TWO

DISCIPLINE WITH WISDOM, DISCERNMENT, AND LOVE

Disciplining our children is one of the most important responsibilities we have as a parent, but it is also one of the most challenging responsibilities. Let us meet the challenge with a wise and loving strategy.

Fresh Ideas for Effectively Changing Your Kids' Behavior

What attributes do you want to see develop in your children as they grow up? Perhaps such noble character qualities as being respectful, hard working, honest, godly, and loving come to mind. Certainly, young people with these strengths would make a positive difference in this world, and the development of these strengths begins in the home, with parents who effectively teach and train their kids to become godly people of character and strength.

Whoa! You may be thinking. *That puts a bit of pressure on us parents, doesn't it?* Never fear! You and I are not alone in our parenting. God is with us. We can look to God to lead us, guide us, and give us the patience, wisdom, and strength we need for the job. As we seek to effectively teach and train our kids in the ways God wants them to live, we must remember that how they turn out is in His hands as well as ours.

The truth is, all kids need training. They don't come into this world naturally knowing how to treat others with respect and love. Our kids must be taught right from wrong; they must be taught the virtues of honesty and integrity. Left to their own devices, they would tend to live reckless, self-centered lives. We all would. So it's our job as parents to lead our kids down a path of honesty, respect, obedience, and love. How do we effect such a positive change in our kids' behavior? Here are four important guidelines for leading your kids in that direction:

1. **Focus on the Lesson You Want to Teach.** The word *discipline* actually means "to teach or train." Keep this definition in the forefront of your mind when your child steps out of line. Then ask yourself, "What am I trying to teach here?" Whenever your child misbehaves, use that discipline opportunity as a teachable moment. Think of discipline not just as a time when you must punish but rather as a time when you are able to teach, train, and help your child be a better person. Often in our anger that they have done something wrong or our frustration that they just don't get it, we forget we are teaching.

2. **Choose a Punishment That Will Effect Change.** Consider what course of action will make your child think, *I'll never do that again* about her infraction. Be pragmatic rather than dogmatic about the punishment you choose, remembering that the same punishment does not fit every disciplinary issue. For instance, Marion put her child in time-out every time she did anything wrong. Marion liked this consequence for misbehavior because it gave her some time to get her daughter out of her way, yet her daughter's behavior showed no signs of improvement. In fact, her daughter probably loved the time she had alone in her room. Marion needed to choose a punishment that was painful for her daughter and that would help her change her behavior. Marion learned that, for punishment to be effective, it must meet certain criteria:

❧ Punishment must hurt. (I'm not talking about physical pain here; I'm referring to a consequence that will make your kids turn from their behavior, like taking away a significant privilege or toy for a certain period of time.)

❧ Punishment must fit the crime and be reasonable.

❧ Punishment must be carried out consistently.

❧ Punishment should be a natural consequence as often as possible.

3. **Discipline in Love, Not Anger.** Your kids will learn life lessons from the way you deliver discipline. If you scream and yell in rage, they will learn to scream and yell to get what they want. If you speak in a loving and firm tone, teaching your kids right from wrong by using an appropriate punishment, then you will teach them positive behavior. When discipline is necessary, give yourself a cooling-down period so you don't lash out at your kids or spew out some ridiculous punishment ("You're grounded for the rest of your life!"). If your children need to be punished for their misbehavior, they'll learn best from that punishment when a caring and respectable adult, not an out-of-control parent, is handling the situation. Also, don't just punish your children.

Talk to them about what you want them to learn from this experience. Then ask your kids to repeat back to you why they are being punished.

4. **Follow Through with the Punishment.** If you tell your children that they can't watch their favorite television show for a week, then keep your word. More importantly, don't create a punishment you don't plan to enforce. It's easy to say, "You can't drive the car for three weeks." But in reality, if you are going to be taking your teen everywhere he needs to go, *his* consequence may become *your* burden, and you'll have trouble following through with the punishment. So think carefully about the ramifications of the punishment you're considering, and then discuss it with your spouse or a friend in order to get a wider perspective. Take your time to discipline your children with wisdom, not foolishly off the top of your head.

How to Train Your Kids from the Inside Out

We parents naturally want our kids to look good on the outside. We want them to act right, look right, and speak right so they fit in, make us proud, and perhaps even glorify God. So we dress them up, we teach them skills and sports, and we help them earn the best grades possible so they will be noted for what they can do. These efforts—these goals—are all well and good, but sometimes in the push to have our kids perform well and look good on the outside, we forget the importance of the inner qualities. Ultimately, we need to be paying attention to the character and heart of our children, not just to the surface issues.

We teach to our kids' hearts by allowing them to see that we are concerned about not only their outward behavior but also the heart behind that behavior. If, for instance, your son were bullying kids at school, you would be doing him a disservice if you focused only on his actions. As you discipline (train) your child, you will want to get to the heart of the problem (pun intended!) and find out why he chose to bully the other kids. Perhaps his actions were based on hate or jealousy or fear. Getting to the core issue, however, doesn't mean allowing your child to get away with what he has done. You will apply punishment, but you will also teach through the punishment. In this example, you will address the importance of respecting other kids and teach your son the value of self-control. You want to help him learn that the issue is not just fighting on the playground, but—more importantly—the issue is being kind and respectful to other people.

Just as a light on your car's dashboard indicates that something is going on inside the car's engine, so your children's behavior and words can be an indicator of something going on inside them as well. When you see that light on the dashboard in your car, do you hit it in an attempt to make it stop shining? No. You check out the problem. You go to the source, whether it is the engine or the brakes. We, too, must go deeper and not simply deal with whatever behavior is showing on the surface of our kids.

Let's say, for instance, that your preteen daughter begins wearing immodest or inappropriate clothes. Instead of yelling at her, telling her that she looks like a tramp, and announcing that she can't wear those kinds of clothes, try a different approach. Go to her and say, "I've noticed you're choosing to wear immodest clothes. Why have you started dressing differently?" Listen to her and then let her know that you love her and that you don't want her to get the wrong kind of attention from boys for the wrong reasons. Talk about the importance of attracting boys who appreciate who she is. Compliment her on who she is; address traits of the heart like her kindness, thoughtfulness, compassion, etc. Then, if you need to, lovingly set boundaries as to what kind of clothing is off-limits.

Finally and most importantly, we teach to our kids' hearts by teaching them to respect God and learn more about His attributes and character. Solomon said, "The fear of the LORD is the beginning of wisdom" (Psalm 111:10 NKJV). If we want our kids to be wise adults, we must teach them a healthy fear of—or respect for—the Lord. The God of the Bible is a loving and compassionate God. He is holy and righteous. He is merciful. Even when our kids are young, we can begin teaching them how the Bible describes God, their heavenly Father.

After all, it is God who changes hearts. He softens us and leads us down a righteous path. God's Word teaches us to love God and love others, and His Spirit is at work in us to help us walk in His ways. You will find more about how to encourage your children's love and understanding of God in Positive Strategy #5 in this book. For now remember that heart change takes place when we teach our kids a healthy respect and love for God and His ways. Obedience happens from the inside out.

Three Essentials for the Mom at Her Wit's End

You've had it. No one warned you that parenting would be this tough. Trust me, all of us moms have had those days. Depending on the personalities of your kids, the number of kids you have, and whether they are boys or girls, you may feel you are at your wit's end when it comes to discipline. So let me offer you three essential tools that you'll want to keep on hand throughout your years as a mother—and, in fact, for life):

1. A Positive Friend or Mentor — When you're feeling down, discouraged, or completely worn out, a friend or mentor can help lift you up. We all need a boost from a friend or a mentor who will give us a new perspective on life when we're frazzled. A parenting mentor or a seasoned mom can help us see the bigger picture and remember that this, too, shall pass. This friend can give us a good word of encouragement or a much-needed listening ear. She can both reassure us that we are normal and help us think through our options. A friend can also help us see that, in the big scheme of life, certain things just aren't worth getting angry or upset over.

2. Patience in the Process — Patience is perhaps one of the most loving gifts we can give our family. Impatience, rage, or anger only stirs things up, often with negative results. A mother's patience—patience when your son needs to be disciplined for the same infraction he's already committed twice this week; patience with your daughter as she struggles through a tough class at school; patience as your kids learn to get along and share with one another—can make a world of difference in the amount of peace and love exhibited in the home.

And we all need God's help and strength if we are to be patient moment by moment. We begin by recognizing the importance of our patience and the tone it sets in the home. Once you decide to work on being more patient and more understanding, you'll be surprised at the amount of patience you will—by God's grace—have for your family.

3. Prayer for Wisdom and Strength — Prayer is a powerful and effective tool for diminishing our worries and helping us overcome our challenges. Often life's circumstances or our children's challenges seem too big to us. We look at a specific situation and think we could never make it through, but prayer turns our eyes upward to the God of hope. As we seek His wisdom and direction, we begin to see that parenting becomes a little easier. As we—with God's help—take bold steps forward, we are able to, bit by bit, move toward solutions. When we cast our cares on Him, our burden doesn't seem so big and overwhelming. Prayer peels away the layers of worry that so easily surround a situation.

These three essential tools for every mom—positive friends, patience, and prayer—are available to every single one of us; we just need to use them. By the way, these tools aren't just for moms who are at their wit's end. These tools are for each one of us, every day, all our life long. As we allow positive friends, patience, and prayer to flourish in our lives, they will result in continual blessings to us and to our family.

If I never correct my child, I am making a nice mess for other folks by and by.

—

Oswald Chambers

POSITIVE

3

Let no unwholesome word
proceed from your mouth,
but only such a word as is
good for edification according
to the need of the moment,
so that it will give grace
to those who hear.

EPHESIANS 4:29 NASB

OPEN UP THE LINES OF COMMUNICATION

Connections are built and bonds are strengthened by good, healthy communication between family members.

What to Say when They Won't Listen

Picture an actress on an evening sitcom talking to her husband. When the conversation becomes ugly, she puts her hands over her ears, closes her eyes, and says, "I'm not listening! La, la, la, la! I can't hear you!" Sadly, this all-too-familiar television scene can also be played out in our homes. Imagine! There are times when our kids just don't want to listen to our wise and profound advice. In fact, sometimes they just want to be left alone, and other times they perceive us as nagging or "always being on their case."

Forcing our kids to listen to us may not achieve the desired results, but if we are wise and gentle, we can open up the lines of communication. So let's explore some ways to open up those lines so we can lovingly converse with our kids. What can we say and do to build that connection? We begin with love.

Hear what the Bible tells us:

Love is patient, love is kind. It does not envy, it does not boast, it is not proud. It is not rude, it is not self-seeking, it is not easily angered, it keeps

no record of wrongs. Love does not delight in evil
but rejoices with the truth. It always protects,
always trusts, always hopes, always perseveres.
Love never fails. (1 Corinthians 13:4–8 NIV)

This kind of love for our kids should be evident in how
we communicate with them. If even some of these traits
characterized our conversations, what we say to our
family members and how we say it, as well as the tone
in our home, might dramatically change. So ask yourself the following questions about how you speak to your
children:

- Am I patient or am I demanding?
- Am I kind or am I rude?
- Is my pride getting in the way of good
communication?
- Am I only thinking about my own needs?
- Am I easily angered?
- Am I keeping a mental record of wrongs?
- Do I protect my kids with my words, or do I harm
them with what I say and/or how I say it?
- Do I build on the trust my kids have earned, or
am I constantly suspicious of them?

❧ Do I speak words of hope and encouragement, or do I discourage my kids?

Answering these questions will help us confront the way we communicate with our kids. We can see ways we may not be communicating with love. Certainly we love our kids, but demonstrating our love in how we communicate can be difficult. Often our own frustrations, expectations, or pride can sneak in and cause us to speak harshly, thereby closing down the lines of communication. With determined effort and help from the Lord, we can speak so that our kids will want to listen.

Remember that it's not only how we say it but also what we say. Think about the difference a few words can make. Let's say your daughter comes home and her new (and, may I add, expensive) backpack has a hole in it. Instead of saying with a stern and accusing voice, "What in the world did you do to your backpack!?" calmly say, "I noticed your backpack has a hole in it. Tell me what happened." This approach shows a desire to understand, and your child will hear your concern rather than feel threatened.

Steer away from phrases like *you always* or *you never* when talking to your kids. When they hear those words, they can immediately feel labeled or boxed in, and they can think you don't see any of their good qualities. So instead of saying, "You never pick up your room. You aren't going anywhere today until it's straightened up," say, "Your room looks so much better when it's straight and neat. You'll need to clean it up before you go out with your friends"—and then follow through! Be sure that the room is neat before any fun with friends begins.

Another technique for drawing our kids in so they will listen to our words is to build on their inter-est and pique their curiosity. Let's say, for instance, it's time to lay down the rules for summer vacation. You could choose to set the kids down on the first day of summer and go over a long list of rules, regulations, and punishments. Sounds fun, huh? Or you could choose to celebrate the first day of summer with a pancake party for breakfast. Make a big poster showing all the things you want to do during the summer. Create a Boredom Buster can and have the kids fill the can with ideas for what to do whenever they feel bored. Finally, go over the few important rules for the summer (how much television a week, what chores each child is responsible for, how much and what kind of computer time will be allowed, etc.), because at that point they're listening!

How to Listen when They Won't Talk

You sense your son is agitated or upset, but you just can't figure out what is going on. When you ask him what's wrong, all he says is, "Nothing." You wish you could draw him out and get to what is bothering him, but you just don't know what to say. All of us parents know the frustration of trying to pull out information from our kids, whether they're hurting, in trouble, or simply quiet.

What are some of the reasons kids won't talk? Here are some possibilities:

- They are angry or hurt.
- They don't quite know how to verbalize what they are feeling.

- ❧❧ They are afraid of being ridiculed, put down, or made to feel ashamed.
- ❧❧ They don't have the time or haven't had the opportunity for a meaningful conversation.
- ❧❧ They simply don't want to open up.

Furthermore, our lives are often so busy running to the kids' activities as well as our own that we have little time for true communication. We must therefore be intentional about making time with our kids, time when they will feel comfortable opening up to us. You may think right away about the time when you are in the car together, but if other kids are in the car or if you're rushed, your child may not feel as though he or she has enough time to tell you what is going on.

Bring your kids out of the silence and into conversation, by creating one-on-one times where conversation can happen more easily. Taking a walk together, visiting a museum, or going to a park or the mall can provide kids with an opportunity to open up and talk with you. When you plan these times, consider what your child enjoys and build on that interest. Recently, for instance, I took my art-loving daughter to a special exhibit at the art museum in our town. It was a great time of talking about her interests, some of her activities, and life in general. What interests your kids? Spend time together time doing things based on their interests.

We must think creatively when it comes to opening up dialogue with our kids. We can write notes to them and encourage them to write out their thoughts to us. We can sit down at the kitchen table with paper and art supplies and then ask our kids to show us how they are feeling or what they are thinking. Sitting outside and looking at the clouds or the stars together can also prompt a relaxed time of conversation. Somehow as we are gazing heavenward together, it's a little easier for kids to open up to us. E-mail offers a good venue too. Kids tend to open up more freely when they are typing an e-mail.

You might even start a cyberspace exchange with a brief e-mail that asks a few questions. Have some fun by giving your kids a quick quiz—and handwritten quizzes work just fine if you aren't comfortable with a computer. A short questionnaire about themselves is pretty painless to answer, and it offers a touch of fun, so use one now and then to encourage your kids to share what is on their mind and heart. Ask them to fill in the blanks in statements such as these:

❧❧ Today I'm feeling _____

_____

because _____

_____.

❧❧ I hope _____.

❧❧ If I weren't at home right now, I'd be _____.

❧❧ I wish Mom would cook _____
for dinner.

❧❧ I'm frustrated about _____.

❧❧ I'm happy about _____.

In addition to the computer desk, another important place for opening up conversation is the family dinner table. Never underestimate the enriching conversation that can happen as you and the kids share a meal together. Studies show that the benefits of families eating together extend far beyond the enjoyable conversation. The more often children and teens experience family dinners together, for example, the less likely they are to use drugs, abuse alcohol, or smoke.[4]

It's important to keep family meals pleasant and uplifting. Don't use dinnertime to address your daily grudges and come down on everyone's case. Instead, enrich conversation by exploring different topics that interest the entire family. For instance, on Sundays you could talk about what each of you learned in church and Sunday school. On Mondays discuss a current event. Tuesday can be a day for asking what is happening at school, on Wednesdays talk about friendships and relationships, and on Thursdays consider sports and hobbies. Perhaps on Friday and Saturday you can talk about family vacations in the past or future.

It's always a good idea to have a few conversation starters handy before you sit down for dinner. Here are a few to help you out—and don't forget to add "Why?"

For Little Ones
- What is your favorite animal at the zoo?
- Who is your favorite person in the Bible?
- Where is your favorite place to visit?

- What do you like best about being at Grandma's house?
- If you could give one toy away to a child who doesn't own any toys at all, what would you give?
- Which of your toys do you wish you could keep forever?

For Older Kids

- If you were the director of a movie, what would the movie be about and whom would you want to star in it?
- What would you name your autobiography?
- If I gave you a free plane ticket to wherever you wanted to go, where would it be?
- What would your dream house look like on the outside?
- How would you decorate your dream house on the inside if money were no object?
- What is one place you wish you could visit in our city that you have never been to before?
- If you had five hours just to yourself to do whatever you want, what would you do?

Your prayer time—at the dinner table and when you tuck the kids in at night—can also allow you to listen to your kids' hearts and hear them express their thoughts both to you and to God. A nighttime routine of praying with your child can become a precious time with your kids until they go to college. Don't miss out on this blessed opportunity to sit down with each of your kids at the end of the day and allow them to open their hearts and share their thoughts. It may take a little extra time and effort on your part, but the results are worth it.

Strengthen Your Kids' Conversational Skills

A young person with good communication skills will go far in life. From childhood friendships and school assignments to job interviews and marriage relationships, people who are able to communicate well have a distinct advantage. Our kids' first classroom of conversation is in their own home with us. As moms, we have the opportunity to teach simple rules of etiquette as well as lifelong lessons of communication that will benefit them for years to come.

Let's take a look at a few basics that we can begin teaching our kids even when they are young:

- **Maintain Eye Contact** — Teach your kids the importance of looking at a person's eyes when they are carrying on a conversation. One technique is to do a little role-playing that will show them how it feels to talk with someone who does not maintain eye contact. Stand face-to-face with your child and tell him he must keep his eyes on you, but you can allow your eyes to wander all over the place. Help him see how rude and uncomfortable it is to try to talk with someone who is looking other places. Also tell him that eye contact shows you are interested. Wandering eyes say you couldn't care less.

- **Listen Well** — Pay attention to what the person is saying. Try to find something you can ask the person about herself or about the topic you're already discussing. Never interrupt.

- **Remember Names** — Repeat a person's name as soon as he tells it to you. Then repeat his name several times during the conversation.

🌸 **Smile** — A genuine smile lets people know you are glad to be talking with them. A smile is a gift you give to the people around you, and it warms them up to you and helps to open up communication.

🌸 **Pass the Ball** — Good conversation is like a good tennis match: you continue to hit the ball (the topic or subject) back and forth. Don't monopolize the conversation or beat a dead ball. Once you have covered one topic, move on to another interest or ask the person a question about herself.

🌸 **Talk about Them, Not Yourself** — Ask questions about the other person's interests. Every person is a unique creation. Find out what people's special passions and talents are by asking opening questions like these:

🌸 What school do you go to?

🌸 What classes are you taking?

🌸 What do you like to do outside of school?

🌸 Do you like sports? art? music?

Good conversation actually comes down to genuinely caring about the person with whom you are talking. So let's teach our kids to take a genuine interest in the people with whom they talk. To help them do that, explain that having a conversation is like being on a treasure hunt. As I said in Positive Strategy #1, every person is a unique treasure chest of wonderful gems waiting to be discovered. When I'm in a conversation with someone, it is my job to use questions and other conversational tools to find those treasures. Try the following role-playing game, called the Treasure Hunt, with your kids—and the more people participating in this game, the better:

Tell the kids that, when you say, "1-2-3-go!" they're supposed to walk around greeting each other as if there is nothing at all important about the other person. They'll see how it feels to be uncared for or unnoticed. It's painful on the giving as well as receiving end.

Next time you say, "Go!" have the kids connect with one person and find a treasure in him or her. Tell them to ask questions like, "What is your favorite food or color or sport?" Encourage everyone to try to find something about this sibling or friend that they didn't know before. Tell the kids to use the conversation hints we learned earlier in this chapter (smile, make eye contact, and bounce conversation back and forth).

After the treasure hunt, invite everyone to sit down and share a gem they learned about the person with whom they were talking. Then ask the participants what they learned about conversation skills. Then help your kids realize that communication is an effective way to show love toward others. The Bible reminds us that "love must be sincere" and to "be devoted to one another in brotherly love. Honor one another above yourselves" (Romans 12:9–10 NIV). Certainly, we love with a sincere love when, in conversations, we truly take a genuine interest in others.

Communication does not begin with being understood, but with understanding others.

—

W. Steven Brown

POSITIVE

4

Come, my children, listen to me; I will teach you the fear of the LORD. Whoever of you loves life and desires to see many good days, keep your tongue from evil and your lips from speaking lies. Turn from evil and do good; seek peace and pursue it.

❧

PSALM 34:11–14 NIV

STRATEGY FOUR

TEACH CHARACTER QUALITIES AND MORAL VALUES

We must anchor our kids in a solid knowledge of God's truth and give them the ability to clearly distinguish between right and wrong. If we leave them to the winds of popular opinion and the current of our society, their ship will sail downstream rapidly.

Teachable Moments Make a Difference

A trip to the zoo. A forgotten homework assignment. A gift for a homeless man. A trophy from a track meet. A lie to a parent. What do these situations have in common? They are among the myriad of teachable moments that typically occur in the life of a family. Lessons about values and character sprout up continually throughout each day, and as we identify them, we can use them to teach our kids moral values. An astute mom recognizes that both pleasant situations and frustrating ones are of value when it comes to passing along a life lesson.

In the Psalms, we read David's prayer: "Teach us to make the most of our time, so that we may grow in wisdom" (Psalm 90:12). We moms can pray a similar prayer: "Lord, help us recognize the opportunities You give us each day to teach our kids valuable lessons, so they will grow in character, integrity, and wisdom." Teachable moments can be far more effective than simply sitting down and discussing the importance of kindness or giving to the poor.

How do you spot a teachable moment? First pray for God's direction. Then begin looking at each encounter and experience as an opportunity for learning. Now don't go around making a lesson out of everything you see and do. You don't want your kids to roll their eyes and, with exasperation, say, "Not another lesson from Mom!" On the other hand, you do want to light a fire for learning as you spark their interest and offer wise words or important life lessons. Here are five everyday occasions that offer a lesson waiting to be taught:

1. **Going Places Together** — Whenever we go somewhere together as a family—on vacation or to a local park, the zoo, a restaurant, the movies—there are opportunities for growth. Patience, self-sacrifice, an appreciation for God as our Creator, and contentment are just a few of the lessons to be learned on a family outing.

2. **Mistakes** — We grow and learn from the "oops" in life. Forgetting, misjudging, or miscalculating can be frustrating and painful, but those times do offer lessons to be learned. We learn, first, that no one is perfect—not us nor anyone we are around. We also learn the importance of forgiveness toward others (because we need it ourselves), being careful, taking responsibility, and not rushing through a task. When your kids

make a mistake, remind them that everyone makes mistakes. Help them see how they can do things differently next time. Most important, try to allow them to experience the natural consequences of their mistakes so they learn from them. From forgotten homework they learn responsibility. From a bad decision they learn to think more carefully next time. Each of us can grow wiser from the times we stumble and fall and pick ourselves up again.

3. **People in Need** — What do you do when you see someone holding out a hand begging for money or food? Do you pass by shaking your head, or do you use it as a teachable moment? You may want to buy some food for the person and even have a conversation. You can teach your kids loving-kindness when you reach out and care for another human being who is hurting. And it's not just the homeless who have needs. A friend may have lost a loved one or experienced a personal struggle. Teach your children how to reach out in compassion to a hurting friend by first join-

ing in prayer for that person and then by talking together as a family about how you can best meet the needs. Finally, allow your kids to participate in the help, thereby giving them hands-on experience in caring for others.

4. **Wins and Losses** — When our children don't perform as well as they'd like and struggle with the pain (whether in sports, piano competition, or grades in school), we can make these teachable moments. First allow your children to grieve and cry over the loss, but eventually help them discover something they can learn from the situation. The lesson may be as basic as we will not win or come out on top in every situation in life. There may be lessons to learn about forgiveness, dealing with anger or jealousy, or creative ways to do things differently next time. Winning can present growth opportunities as well. Lessons about being gracious and thoughtful of the other contestants can be prompted by a win, as well as lessons in pride versus humility and in thanking God for the abilities and talents He has provided.

5. Discipline — It may seem like a negative setting for a teachable moment, but we can't overlook the opportunity to teach and train our children whenever we must discipline them. When our child is caught in a lie or an untruth, we have the occasion to teach the importance of honesty. When our kids disobey, we help them learn the responsibility of obedience not only through our punishment but also with our words. When a son or daughter speaks disrespectfully either to you or to another person, it is your chance to teach about respect and kindness. Don't look at disciplining your child as a huge frustration. Instead see it as an opportunity to help your child learn important life lessons.

Martin Luther said, "Family life is a school for character."[5] Consider every occasion in your family's life together as a great occasion to teach your children values and character. And the more time you spend hanging out with your kids, the more you can take advantage of these moments. Never underestimate the importance of the precious time you spend together and of the teaching opportunities that will emerge.

Books, Movies, Music, and More Can Be Tools

In *The Jesus I Never Knew*, author Philip Yancey tells about a rather odd revival that broke out in the Soviet Union during the 1970s while the country was still under Communist rule. Here's what Yancey reports:

> In the early 1970s Malcolm Muggeridge was surprised to hear that members of the intellectual elite in the Soviet Union were experiencing a spiritual revival. Anatoli Kuznetsov, living in exile in England, told him there was scarcely a single writer or artist or musician in the U.S.S.R. who was not exploring spiritual issues. Muggeridge said, "I asked him how this could have happened, given the enormous anti-religious brainwashing job done on the citizenry, and the absence of all Christian literature, including the Gospels. His reply was memorable; the authorities, he said, forgot to suppress the works of Tolstoy and Dostoevsky, the most perfect expositions of the Christian faith of modern times."[6]

Amazing! The powerful influence books have in transforming people's lives. God can use all forms of the media to communicate messages of hope and redemption and to teach moral values and character. Many a leader has been inspired to greatness through the stories that were read to them as children. William F. Russell writes in *Classics to Read Aloud to Your Children*, "There is a whole world of good writing, good reading, and good listening awaiting your children—a world that you can open up to them and one that they will enjoy for the rest of their lives. What better gift can there possibly be?"[7]

Russell recommends not only reading to your children when they are young but continuing the practice even through their middle-school years. Read a variety of fables, poetry, stories, and biographies to give your children a rich heritage of insight through literature. Former secretary of education William J. Bennett has compiled several great resources for parents who desire to teach their children values through literature. *The Book of Virtues* and *The Moral Compass* (Simon & Schuster) are both chock-full of powerful stories that provide moral education.

Whenever you read with your kids, ask them thought-provoking questions like, "What do you think Tom Sawyer learned from his actions?" or "How might we apply the lesson from this fable to our life?" Help your kids personalize and internalize the lessons they learn from stories. And check out *Books That Build Character* (Touchstone) by William Kilpatrick for a reference that will lead you to great literature for your kids.

Movies and the visual arts also greatly influence our society today. Several excellent resources are available to help you not only make wise decisions about what your children watch but also to encourage you to teach moral values using the movie as a source of discussion. One of my favorite resources is Feature Films for Families (www.familytv.com), a company committed to providing quality entertainment that strengthens the traditional values you want for your family. They work to unite concerned people everywhere into an effective voice that will make the world a better place.

You may find www.Movieguide.org another helpful resource for your family. Movieguide is a ministry dedicated to redeeming the values of the mass media according to biblical principles by both influencing entertainment industry executives and helping families make wise media choices. Another Web site you may find helpful is www.teachwithmovies.org, a unique tool for both parents and teachers that promotes character education through films. And I probably don't need to say this, but before showing a movie to your kids always review it first to make sure it fits your own family values.

When you watch films with your family, you can do more than just enjoy the closeness and blessing of time together. You can also provide opportunities for discussion. You may choose to go for ice cream after the movie in order to provide a delightful time of discussion. Jot down a few questions you want to bring up after the movie. Don't make the after-movie discussion too lengthy. Instead of asking a long list of questions, narrow the focus of the conversation to just one or two moral values you want to use the movie to reinforce.

Sometimes you may want to stretch beyond your normal boundaries. For instance, when *The Patriot* came out, our daughters were in middle school. The movie is rated R, but we knew from reading the reviews that it teaches several values like courage and the sacrifice our forefathers made for our present freedom. We wanted our girls to see the movie even though it was a little violent, and watching the movie together provided the opportunity for a valuable and insightful family discussion. Other movies such as *Gladiator*, *The Count of Monte Cristo*, and *Braveheart* were also a little outside our normal range of acceptability for our young teens, but we watched the movies together as a family and talked about moral and value lessons afterward.

For younger kids, *VeggieTales* (Big Idea Productions), *Superbook* (Tyndale House Publisers), *Story Keepers* (Zondervan Publishers), and *Hermie and Friends* (by Max Lucado, Thomas Nelson Publishers) offer delightful value-based and biblical education. All are available at your local Christian bookstore. *McGee and Me, The Chronicles of Narnia*, and *Adventures in Odyssey* are great teaching tools for elementary-age kids.

Like the books and movies in our world, music can greatly influence our kids. Music not only calms the spirit, but it can teach through its words as well. As an avid listener of Christian radio, I know my soul has been refreshed and my faith strengthened through Christian music. My kids have grown to love the music as well. When my kids were young, we listened to fun Bible songs and character-building music such as *Wee Sing Bible Songs*. Visit www.songsforteaching.com or www.cherylmelody. com for other character-building music.

The possibilities for teaching values are infinite! You can creatively use Christian magazines for kids (visit www.fotf.org), puppet shows (www.kidbiz.com), games (www.familyfun.com), or even fun activities with friends. A number of years ago, several friends and I saw the need for an after-school club to teach character values. We started a group called USA Sonshine Girls, and its purpose was to bring young girls together to learn and then reinforce biblical character qualities. We met twice a month, once to teach the children a character quality and the second time to go on a field trip and live out the value we had learned. It was a fun way to teach our kids values as well as a deeper love for the Lord.[8]

Teach Your Kids to Be Good Citizens

Not too long ago I ran across a retro-looking book, and on the cover was the image of a clean-cut young man holding his hand over his heart. The book was entitled *The Good Citizen's Handbook: A Guide to Proper Behavior*. In the introduction, the author begins with this delightful description:

> A GOOD CITIZEN is well-groomed and fun to be around. She's trustworthy, helpful, courteous, and kind. He's loyal, thrifty, clean, and brave. Good Citizens beware delinquency and obey even minor laws. They tend their yards, brush their teeth in a circular motion, vote in every election, and always try their best. They know, as R.O. Hughes points out in the 1930s textbook *Elementary Community Civics*, "The character of any community, however large or small, depends upon the character of its members. Every good

citizen in the community is a good influence. Every evil citizen is a bad influence."[9]

Certainly in our society today we have slid far from the respectful and caring values of the 1930s. Despite the current of our culture, we moms can still make a difference by first making a difference in our homes. It's never too late to raise decent citizens who uphold and live out strong moral values.

What does it take to be a good citizen? Let's examine a few vital ingredients of fine citizens and strong leaders for the next generation. A good citizen:

❧ Honors God, Country, and Others — When we honor someone, we speak well of that person. In honoring God we glorify Him and reverence Him. To honor our country means we are loyal to its high ideals. Honoring a person means giving respect to that individual. We are loyal with our words and actions. We live in such a way that we do not dishonor God's name, our country's values, or other people's rights to life, liberty, and the pursuit of happiness.

❧ Respects Others — Showing respect for other people begins with basic kindness, grounded in the recognition that every person is a beloved creation of God. We show respect not only with our words but also through our actions. We respect other people's property by taking care of it, not damaging or harming it. We show respect for our neighbors by keeping a neat yard, and we show respect for our family by keeping a clean home. When we give respect to people, we show appreciation and consideration for them as well as their property.

❧ Serves the Community — President John F. Kennedy said, "Ask not what your country can do for you, but what you can do for your country." Good citizens are not looking for what they can get, but rather what they can give to help their community. Whether in your church community, your neighborhood, or the city where you live, you can always find opportunities to volunteer and offer help. An individual citizen's heart for service is foundational to a strong society.

Obeys the Rules — A good citizen is obedient to God first and to country second. God has given us commandments, not for our detriment but for our betterment! Anarchy (life with no rules) breeds chaos. God's commandments and our country's laws (based on those biblical principles) help create a strong structure on which a great country can be built. We participate in that building project when, as good citizens, we follow our nation's rules.

As helpful as these four guidelines are, the entire scope of being a good citizen can ultimately be reduced to the following two commands:

- Love God with all your heart, soul, and mind.
- Love other people as you love yourself. (see Matthew 22:37–40)

These two commands sum up every command given by God or rule established by man. We must teach our kids to live lives filled with love for God and love for others.

When we do so, we are encouraging them to be good citizens. Being a good citizen may be considered a dying art, yet a crucial factor in the foundation of society. As we parents faithfully teach our kids to value the characteristics of honor, respect, service, and obedience, we can make a difference in this world beginning with our family.

Values are the foundation of our character and of our confidence. A person who does not know what he stands for or what he should stand for will never enjoy true happiness or success.

—

Lionel Kendrick

POSITIVE

5

Love the Lord your God with
all your heart and with all your
soul and with all your strength.
These commandments that I
give you today are to be upon
your hearts. Impress them on
your children.

❧

DEUTERONOMY 6:5–7 NIV

HELP YOUR KIDS DEVELOP AN INTIMACY WITH GOD

God mandates that parents—not churches or schools—be our children's spiritual teachers. We have the divine responsibility of leading them to a saving knowledge of God and encouraging them in their love for God.

Encouraging a Love for God's Word

Throughout our nation's history, many great Americans have held the Bible in high esteem, recognizing the value of its redeeming truth and eternal wisdom for our daily lives.[10]

George Washington said, "It is impossible to rightly govern the world without God and the Bible."

Abraham Lincoln commented, "I am profitably engaged in reading the Bible. Take all of this Book upon reason that you can, and the balance by faith, and you will live and die a better man."

Woodrow Wilson said to an audience, "I have a very simple thing to ask of you. I ask every man and woman in this audience that from this day on they will realize that part of the destiny of America lies in their daily perusal of this great Book."

Helen Keller is quoted as saying, "Unless we form the habit of going to the Bible in bright moments as well as in trouble, we cannot fully respond to its consolations, because we lack equilibrium between light and darkness."

Douglas MacArthur said, "Believe me, sir, never a

night goes by, be I ever so tired, but I read the Word of God before I go to bed."

Henry Ford claimed, "All the sense of integrity, honor, and service I have in my heart I got from hearing the Bible read by a school teacher in the three years I was privileged to go to a little, old-fashioned grammar school. The teacher read the Bible every morning to start the day right. I got a great deal out of that influence."

If we were to take all the comments people have made throughout history as to the redeeming value of God's Word, I suppose they would fill numerous volumes. The Bible has indeed been the inspiration of many great leaders, and it can be our source of inspiration, strength, and guidance every day. We want our children to grow up to know the importance of God's Word and the powerful effect it can have on their lives.

We read in 2 Timothy 3:16–17 that "all Scripture is inspired by God and is useful to teach us what is true and to make us realize what is wrong in our lives. It straightens us out and teaches us to do what is right. It is God's way of preparing us in every way, fully equipped for every good thing God wants us to do" (NLT). I'm guessing you want your kids to be fully equipped for every good thing

God wants them to do. I know that's what I want for my kids! So we must be deliberate about building in our kids a genuine love and passionate desire for God's Word.

First, you can begin by showing your kids how much you love and respect the Bible. Allow your kids to see you reading and studying God's Word. Tell them what you've learned from the Bible and how it affects you. Talk about its truths in daily conversation. You may want to say something like, "I love the Bible. It teaches me about the wonderful love God has for me and for you." Or perhaps, "Today I read the most amazing story about courage and faith…" The Bible is not just a book full of rules and regulations; it is instead a treasure chest full of encouragement, strength, truth, reassurance, guidance, and hope.

Second, read the Bible daily with your kids while they are young. Choose a consistent time when you can read together. There are many children's Bibles available today. Visit a Christian bookstore to find one that suits your kids' ages and interests. Don't force a lengthy, uncomfortable Bible-reading time on your kids. Gently, lovingly lead them to the refreshing beauty of God's Word and help them enjoy the blessings of hearing the wonderful truth-filled stories and life-giving principles found in the Bible.

Your goal is to help your children develop the habit of reading God's Word and, eventually, of reading it on their own. When you see they are ready to start reading the Bible for themselves, you may want to help them pick out a youth or teen Bible to call their own. We moms can spark an interest in God's Word while our kids are young and fan the flame as they get older. Our hope is for our kids to shine brightly as they live out and speak the truth they discover during their own study of the Bible.

The great preacher Charles H. Spurgeon says this about the power of his own mother's influence on his life:

> I cannot tell how much I owe to the solemn words and prayer of my good mother. It was the custom on Sunday evenings, while we were children, for her to stay at home with us. We sat around the table and read verse by verse, while she explained the Scripture to us. After that was done, then came the time of pleading with God. Some of the words of our mother's prayers we shall never forget, even when our

heads are gray. I remember her once praying thus: "Now, Lord, if my children go on in sin, it will not be from ignorance that they perish, and my soul must bear a swift witness against them at the day of judgment if they lay not hold of Jesus Christ."[11]

May we be faithful—just as Spurgeon's mother was—in teaching our kids the treasures and truths of God's wonderful and glorious Word!

Four Basic Truths about Prayer Every Child Needs to Learn

How blessed are the children of a praying mom! We see an example in the life of Spurgeon, and many of us see the benefits in our own life. A praying mom worries less. A praying mom walks in faithful confidence. A praying mom looks to God for direction and trusts Him for her kids' future. A praying mom encourages her kids to be praying kids because she shows them through her example and teaches from her experience.

Certainly we want to raise children who love to pray. So how do we start? There are four basic truths we need to teach and tell our kids about prayer, so they can grow to love and practice the discipline of prayer in their own life. These truths are important to pass along to our children, but they are important for us to know as well. Allow the following insights about prayer to penetrate your heart and renew your mind:

1. **God Wants Us to Go to Him in Prayer** — Throughout God's Word we see a beautiful invitation to go to God and cast our cares on Him. His voice beckons us to bring our praise, thanksgiving, confessions, and requests to His throne. Listen to what Jesus said about prayer: "Keep on asking, and you will be given what you ask for. Keep on looking, and you will find. Keep on knocking, and the door will be opened.... If you sinful people know how to give good gifts to your children, how much more will your heavenly Father give good gifts to those who ask him" (Matthew 7:7, 11). In the Old Testament, God told His people if they humbled themselves and prayed, then He would hear their prayers and heal the land. In the New Testament, the apostle

Paul encouraged believers to pray about everything and to pray without ceasing. King David encouraged his people to "trust in [God] at all times. Pour out your heart to him, for God is our refuge" (Psalm 62:8). It is tempting to think that God is too great or too busy or too frustrated with us to want to listen to our prayers, but nothing could be further from the truth. God continually calls us to Himself as He holds His arms open wide.

2. **God Hears His People's Prayers** — Not only does God want us to pray, but the Bible also reassures us that He hears our prayers. To think that the High King of heaven bends His ear to hear our voice! King David knew that truth: "The LORD hears his people when they call to him for help. He rescues them from all their troubles" (Psalm 34:17). The apostle John wrote, "We can be confident that he will listen to us whenever we ask him for anything in line with his will" (1 John 5:14). The writer of Hebrews reminds us that, through Jesus, we can "come boldly to the throne of our gracious God. There

we will receive his mercy, and we will find grace to help us when we need it" (Hebrews 4:16). So let us go to God, believing that He hears us and knowing that He is able to work in ways beyond what we can ask or imagine.

3. **God Deserves the Praises of His People** — It is easy to get in the request mode when we go to the Lord in prayer: "Lord, bless this and, Lord, bless that." But we want to teach our kids that prayer is a conversation with God, a time for praising Him and listening for His voice, not simply a time for making requests. When we realize we are coming before the Most Holy God, we can't help but want to pour out praise for who He is and what He can accomplish. As we teach our kids to pray, let's have them begin by praising God. After all, we wouldn't think about walking into the throne room of a great king and immediately start spewing out requests. Instead we would first pay our respects to the ruler. If we would honor an earthly king with such respect, how much more should we honor the King of kings and Lord of lords?

Your prayers may begin like this: "Wonderful, merciful God, we praise You because You are sovereign. You are holy. You are our Rock and our Refuge. You know all things, and You can do all things. We come to You as sinners in need of forgiveness, and we know that, through Your Son's death on the cross, we are forgiven. Thank You for hearing our prayers. Thank You for Your marvelous grace. We come to You now with our requests…" When we begin with praise, we remind ourselves of how great God is, our faith is strengthened, and our spirit is uplifted. As Psalm 92:1 reminds us, "It is good to give thanks to the LORD, to sing praises to the Most High"

4. **God Responds to Our Prayers** — We may think because we didn't get exactly what we asked for, God didn't answer us. Not so! We must rejoice in the fact that our all-knowing and all-loving heavenly Father does not respond affirmatively to every request we make of Him. Instead, as a wise and kind Father, He responds with a yes, no, or wait based on His perspective of

eternity. You don't give your children everything they ask you for, do you? I'm sure your answer is no. And we moms say no because our kids don't always know what is best for them. In our loving wisdom, we do what we know is best, and that means we don't say yes to everything. C. S. Lewis once said, "If God had granted all the silly prayers I've made in my life, where should I be now?"[12] I am eternally grateful that God answers according to His will and not my whim.

God may not answer our prayers the way or in the timeframe we wish He would, but Scripture assures us that our prayers are effective and that we are to continue praying. Jesus used a parable about a persistent woman asking a judge for justice to remind us to be persistent in prayer (Luke 18:1–8), and Jesus told His disciples, "You can ask for anything in my name, and I will do it, because the work of the Son brings glory to the Father. Yes, ask anything in my name, and I will do it" (John 14:13, 14). Asking in Jesus' name means we are asking according to His will. So let's be faithful to ask not according to our own will but according to His—and then let's trust Him for His loving response.

There is no better way to get to know someone than to spend time in conversation with that person, and the same is true of God. Our kids will grow in their love for God as they spend time with Him in prayer. As you can see, prayer goes beyond simply thanking God for dinner. Prayer is a response to an invitation, to the almighty God's invitation to commune with Him, the Creator and Sovereign King of heaven and earth.

Fun Ideas for Scripture Memory

Memorizing verses from the Bible can have a powerful effect on our daily lives. As we come to know His Word and hide it in our hearts, it gives us strength, hope, and joy when we face the cares of the world. The writer of Hebrews said, "The word of God is full of living power. It is sharper than the sharpest knife, cutting deep into our innermost thoughts and desires. It exposes us for what we really are" (Hebrews 4:12). And King David, a man after God's own heart, said, "I have hidden your word in my heart, that I might not sin against you" (Psalm 119:11).

Now I know you're thinking that you'd like to memorize Scripture and teach your kids to do the same, but it seems so difficult. Well, it doesn't have to be. In fact, memorizing Scripture can actually be fun! As God gives you the desire to learn His Word, He will also give you the ability to hide His Word in your heart. Let's consider a few creative ways to make God's Word come alive in our brains. Our simple strategy will be: "See it. Say it. Do it."

See It — Begin by writing out the memory verse on a large index card. Here are a few verses you may want to memorize together as a family at a pace of one passage per week:

Week One: Proverbs 3:5, 6

Week Two: Psalm 19:14

Week Three: Matthew 22:37, 38

Week Four: Ephesians 4:29

Week Five: 1 Peter 5:6, 7

Week Six: 2 Peter 1:3

Week Seven: Romans 5:8

Week Eight: Romans 8:28

As you write out the verse for the week, use different colors for different phrases. (Did you know that people tend to memorize better in color rather than in black and white?) You may also want to group certain phrases or words together as you write out the verse. After you've written the verse, draw pictures to fit the verse or cut out pictures from a magazine. Sometimes the sillier the picture the better. For instance, once when I was memorizing a verse beginning with "Let us…" I drew a head of lettuce to help me remember how it started.

It is a good idea to write the verse on several cards. Doing so will help you get familiar with the verse, but you can also distribute the verse cards around the house where you and your family members will see them often. Place one in the car and one in your purse as well. I usually put one on my bathroom mirror and one near my kitchen sink, so I will run across them in my daily routine. I've also found that writing the verse helps me memorize it better than typing it out, and that may be true for you too. Encourage your kids to design their own creative verse cards. Or you might also work together to create one big, colorful poster of the verse for display in the kitchen or family room. I use the flipping photo albums (available at many retail shops where frames are sold), and I insert a new index card for each verse. Then I can easily flip back through to review the verses I've been learning.

Another way to see a verse is through hand motions or acting it out. If a verse starts with the word "For," begin by holding up four fingers. Then try to use as many hand motions and signals as possible to help the verse sink in. It's fun to work on hand motions together as a family because it brings in everyone's creativity. Then you can enjoy saying and motioning the verse together. Finally, you may want to regularly and system-atically review the scripture you have memorized. Think about designating every Sunday evening as a scripture review time.

Say It — It's one thing to memorize a verse in your head; it's another thing to say it aloud to the people around you. But saying the verse out loud to one another helps establish and seal a verse in your brain. Don't worry if you stumble and need to peek at the card at first. Just keep trying until you get it—and encourage your family members to say their verses to one another. Also, look for opportunities during the week to use the verse in conversation with anther person. I know that when I'm memorizing a Bible verse, it's at the forefront of my heart and mind, so I usually find it pretty easy to bring it up in conversation when I'm having lunch with a friend or I see someone who could use an encouraging word.

As you practice a verse together as a family, you may want to play the Soft to Loud Game. Start by forming a circle and bending at the knees so you are low to the ground. In a very soft whisper, say the verse together. Next, begin to straighten up a little and say the verse a little louder than a whisper. Now, almost standing, say the verse in a volume just below normal. Then stand straight and use your normal volume. Next, raise your hands above your head and shout the verse. Then, jumping up as high as you can, shout the verse one more time—and you can work back down to a whisper if you want. By playing this simple game, you end up saying the verse at least six times together.

If you have a mini-trampoline (the kind used for home exercise), you can give the kids each a turn to jump on the trampoline and say the verse while they are jumping. Allow the kids to take additional turns so they say the verse several times. You can also practice the verse while you are swinging at the park. You may also want to try a family lineup. Stand in a line and have the first person in line say just the first part of the verse or maybe even just one word. The next person in line must continue the verse, and this continues on down the line. You may want to go through the line several times or change positions every time you come to the end of the verse. If your family is musically inclined, you could also put the verse to music. Choose a familiar tune that works with the verse.

Do It — Now that you have *seen* the verse and *said* the verse, it's time to *do* the verse. Come up with ways to live out the verse in your life. Perhaps, for instance, you've memorized "Trust in the LORD with all your heart and lean not on your own understanding; in all your ways acknowledge him, and he will make your paths straight" (Proverbs 3:5, 6 NIV). Make it your mission during the week to look for opportunities to acknowledge God and to choose to trust Him. What are you worried about? Choose to trust Him instead. Is there a decision you need to make, but you want to lean on your own understanding instead of seeking God and His guidance?

Apply the verse to your life right now—and encourage your kids to do the same. At the end of the week, come together as a family and share your opportunities and stories. You may even want to record in a journal how you put your memory verse into action.

With every new verse you work on, pray and ask the Lord to help you apply the principles in His Word, and He will open your eyes to opportunities. You will be amazed at how He opens the door to applications of the Scripture verses you are hiding in your heart. So be careful the week you memorize 1 Peter 5:6, the verse about being humble! 🌺

*The greatest desire of my heart for my sons was
that they might become the servants of God.*
— Charles H. Spurgeon

POSITIVE

6

In the same way, let your light shine before men, that they may see your good deeds and praise your Father in heaven.

MATTHEW 5:16 NIV

STRATEGY SIX

BE A POSITIVE ROLE MODEL

Our children look to us to learn how to act and how to live. Our words may teach, but our life example shouts.

No One Is Perfect

Dwight L. Moody told the story of a blind man who lived in a large city. He would sit on a street corner with his lantern beside him. A passerby noticed the strange sight and asked the man why he needed the lantern since he was blind. The old man replied, "The lantern is for other people, so they will not stumble over me." Like the blind man, we parents desire to hold a light up for our kids to help illumine the way they should go. May we do that by our example. May we live in such a way that we do not make our kids stumble.

Our living example may be the most powerful tool for teaching and training our kids. I've seen that truth illustrated in my own home as I've watched each of my daughters become like a little me. That's good in many ways—and a little scary in others. Seeing that my girls have followed my example underscores the fact that our children may or may not understand the wise words we say, but our example is always clear to them. How we act and live shouts a message loud and clear to the members of our family.

Juvenile court judge Leo B. Blessing said, "The foundations of character are built not by lecture, but by bricks of good example, laid day by day."[13] How do we lay a good foundation for our kids through our example when we are not always very good people? As an imperfect mom like you (and every other mom on the planet), I want to encourage you that when we are weak, God is strong and able to help us. Certainly, we must strive for excellence in our example, but we must also remember that God gives us strength to be the moms—the examples—He wants us to be. Furthermore, He is a redeeming God who can use even our mistakes and our weaknesses for a greater purpose.

Case in point…

One of my favorite people in the Bible is Peter, a bold fisherman with an impetuous personality. Without a doubt he made a few mistakes along the way, and he said a few things he shouldn't have said. God used Peter in a mighty way, to build His church, it is quite obvious from reading the Gospels that Peter was far from perfect. He wrote, "As we know Jesus better, his divine power gives us everything we need for living a godly life. He has called us to receive his own glory and goodness" (2 Peter 1:3). What a marvelous truth! We may not have what it takes to live as we should, but as we come to know Jesus better, His divine power gives us everything we need to live the life He calls us to.

The power of our own example to influence our children—for good or bad—may seem overwhelming, but be encouraged. I'll say it again: you are not perfect, but you are not alone in your parenting. God is with you and is able to help you be the teacher and the example you need to be. Consider what lessons your kids are currently learning from your example. Take a moment to ponder what you are teaching your kids by the way you live and act. What are a few areas that need to change? What do you want your kids to see that isn't there right now? Ask God to help you see yourself honestly as you answer these questions.

Now consider what life in your family would be like if, moment by moment, day in and day out, your kids saw in you the traits of love, joy, peace, patience, kindness, goodness, faithfulness, gentleness, and self-control? Would you be content to have them learn these nine traits from your example? Perhaps you are thinking, *Well, it would be nice if my kids learned those qualities from my example, but I can't consistently live out those qualities in my daily life.* I have good news for you, fellow mom! The Bible says these nine qualities are the fruit of God's Spirit, and His Spirit at work in you can produce these qualities.

Jesus Himself said that as we abide in Him and He abides in us, we will bear much fruit, but without Him we can do nothing (John 15:1–5). Do you want to live a fruitful life, rich in the fruit of God's Spirit? That kind of life happens when you're in relationship with Him. Remember what good ol' Peter said: "As we know Jesus better, his divine power gives us everything we need for living a godly life." Our relationship with God begins when we, in faith, acknowledge that Jesus is the Son of God and that He died on the cross to pay for my sins and yours.

Our relationship with God grows and develops as we read His Word and spend time with Him in prayer. In the spiritual realm as well as in the natural world, fruit is not produced from dead or severed branches. Fruit is produced from branches that are attached to the vine. Jesus declared that He is the vine and we are the branches. And so, dear mother, the key to our being good examples for our kids is not our own perfection, but our seeking a deeper relationship with God and growing in Him.

Qualities Your Kids Need to See in You

When Patty came home from school hurt and angry, her mother asked her what was bothering her. Fighting back tears, Patty described her devastating day at school. All the girls had been talking about the party they had gone to at Sarah's house over the weekend. Patty honestly felt that she was the only girl in the entire grade who hadn't been invited. At first she was understandably hurt, but then anger at Sarah grew within her. Patty wasn't sure how she was going to do it, but she was going to get even with Sarah—and she would never be Sarah's friend again!

Patty's mom recognized immediately that Patty was moving in the wrong direction. She sat down next to Patty on her bed and began to talk with her about the importance of forgiveness and not seeking revenge. She even quoted verses from the Bible to make her point. Patty listened, but then she asked her mom, "Why should I listen to what you say about forgiveness? For years you've detested Mrs. Byrd down the street because she hurt your feelings. And you always talk about how angry you are at your parents because of the way they treated you." Patty sarcastically added, "Yeah, I can see that forgiveness is real important in your life!"

If only teenagers weren't so truthful! Patty had pegged her mother. If forgiveness is so vital for us as Christians, why hadn't Peggy's mom shown it? Peggy was right in wanting her daughter to forgive Sarah, but her lesson would have been better received if she had lived out forgiveness in her own life.

Forgiveness, integrity, and humility are three essential principles we want our children to live by, yet these three principles are difficult to live out in our own lives. My purpose here is not to convict but rather to inspire you. We moms must, by God's strength and grace, do our best to live out these qualities in our home. Let's briefly examine each one of these three essentials, traits that are not highly esteemed in the media or by society at large.

Forgiveness — Forgiveness is important to God. In fact, it is so important that Jesus said in His Sermon on the Mount, "If you forgive those who sin against you, your heavenly Father will forgive you. But if you refuse to forgive others, your Father will not forgive your sins" (Matthew 6:14, 15). Whoa! Now that's a bit strong, isn't it? But if we honestly recognize our sin and remember that we are forgiven completely through Christ, we will respond by forgiving others. If we are not willing to forgive others, we may not truly recognize how much we have been forgiven; we may not be living under the grace of God.

So, whenever we ask for God's forgiveness, we should be asking ourselves, "Have I forgiven the people around me?" Sometimes the little things—a hurtful word, an unreturned phone call, a snub from someone at church—make us hold a grudge. The Bible tells us that we must (yes, that was the word *must*) forgive others because, through Christ, we have been forgiven of everything. May I therefore encourage you to dwell each day on the beauty of God's forgiveness and to ask Him to help you forgive others. One more word: Forgiveness doesn't mean you allow someone to continue to walk all over you. Set boundaries if necessary, but release the right to hold something over another person.

Integrity — If we are to be positive role models for our kids, integrity must characterize every part of our lives. Our kids must hear truth in our words, see truth in our actions, and understand truth through our consistent example. Yet integrity seems to be at an all-time low in our society. When our kids see adults—from corporate executives to teachers in the classroom—living dishonest lives, it's no wonder that cheating is rampant at schools and teenage crime is increasing. Even certain preachers say one thing and do another. Our kids need to see examples of truth and honesty—and they definitely need to find you being an example in their own home.

If children see their parents cheating on taxes, lying to a neighbor, or stealing from the workplace, they get the clear message that honesty doesn't matter. When parents model a lack of integrity, kids learn to do what is right in their own eyes; whatever benefits them is the rule they follow. When people live as they please instead of living in the parameters of honesty, they become their own god. On the other hand, if we live out our own healthy reverence and fear of God, our integrity will shine forth, and our kids will see it.

Be aware that if we only teach integrity with our words, but we don't live it out in front of our kids, the spoken lesson is completely null and void. So may God help us each and every day to consistently lead a life characterized by honesty and truth and uprightness. The soundness of the next generation depends on it.

Humility — It may come as a surprise to you to find humility among the three essentials our kids need to see in our lives. After all, a humble spirit is not usually the hottest trend or the most talked-about pursuit in either secular or Christian circles. Yet, understood correctly and lived out in God's power, humility is a powerful and beautiful quality.

What *is* true humility? It isn't cowering from people and allowing ourselves to be doormats. It isn't walking around with our head down saying, "I'm awful. I'm no good." Humility is rooted in reverence for God and the realization that all I have comes from Him. The opposite of humility is pride or arrogance; it's a focus on one's own greatness. The Bible reminds us that pride goes before a fall (Proverbs 16:18). Pride says, "It's not my fault. I don't need to apologize. I deserve all that I have." Humility says, "I will take an open-eyed, realistic view of my own humanity." Humble people apologize when necessary, and they do not live with a sense of entitlement. Humble people are also confident—confident in the gifts God has given them.

Why, then, is it so important for our kids to see humility in us? To begin with, a prideful mom breeds contempt in her children, for she feels she knows it all, she will not back down from her viewpoint, and of course she never says she's sorry. A humble mom, however, recognizes that learning is part of the parenting experience. She is not above apologizing when she loses her temper or has made an error. Kids need to learn how to apologize, and home is the first learning ground. There are times in all of our lives when we must admit that we don't know it all and that we are fallible.

The most beautiful truth that humility brings to our life is the fact that God has given us our abilities, our talents, and our skills. Prideful people may waste these gifts on selfish gain, but humble people use their gifts and talents to honor God and to make a positive difference in the world. We may never see a magazine cover touting "5 Easy Steps to Humility," but be assured that the walk you take toward humility will help teach your kids a key to great success in life.

Goals, Not Regrets

When I was a track coach, I taught my runners to keep their eyes on the finish line. "Look to the finish. Don't turn your head to look back, or you'll lose the race," I told the kids. The Bible encourages us to do the same. We're to keep our eyes on the goal and not waste time looking back. The apostle Paul, whose sordid pre-Christian past involved killing Christians, later wrote, "No, dear brothers and sisters, I am still not all I should be, but I am focusing all my energies on this one thing: Forgetting the past and looking forward to what lies ahead, I strain to reach the end of the race and receive the prize for which God, through Christ Jesus, is calling us up to heaven" (Philippians 3:13, 14).

I know you may have regrets about what you have done or how you have lived in the past. (We all do!) So I want to encourage you, fellow mom, to not dwell on the past or waste time wallowing in regret. Apologize if necessary, but move forward in a new and positive direction. Just as God had a great plan for Paul's life—enabling him to encourage and strengthen the Christians in the early church—God has a great plan for you as you raise your family. In a way, Paul was parenting like you are as he raised the baby Christians and nurtured them in their walk of faith. Paul could have become discouraged if he'd dwelled on his past mistakes, but he made a conscious decision to move forward on the path God had for him.

We must move forward as well, with our eyes on the goal of being a consistent and positive role model for our kids. More importantly, we must keep our eyes on Christ who will enable us to reach that goal. On our own, we may not be able to produce the fruit of love, joy, and peace in our lives, but God's Spirit at work in us can. We may have the ability to consistently live out forgiveness, integrity, and humility, but God can give us what we need to do just that.

In Hebrews we read about a great race, and we are the runners. Yes, you and me! Read about it here:

> Since we are surrounded by such a huge crowd of witnesses to the life of faith, let us strip off every weight that slows us down, especially the sin that so easily hinders our progress. And let us run with endurance the race that God has set before us. We do this by keeping our eyes on Jesus, on whom our faith depends from start to finish. He was willing to die a shameful death on the cross because of the joy he knew would be his afterward. Now he is seated in the place of highest honor beside God's throne in heaven.
> (Hebrews 12:1, 2)

As we run this race of life, little ones in our home are watching to see how we do it. So let's get rid of any sin that may be weighing us down, and then let's run with our eyes fixed on Jesus, the Author and Finisher of our faith. Yes, the race is tough, and it requires endurance and strength, but we do not run alone. God's Spirit is able to strengthen us day by day. As we read in Isaiah, "Those who wait on the LORD will find new strength. They will fly high on wings like eagles. They will run and not grow weary. They will walk and not faint" (40:31).

The secret of home rule is self-rule, first being ourselves what we want our children to be.

—

Andrew Murray

POSITIVE

7

The father of a righteous man has great joy; he who has a wise son delights in him. May your father and mother be glad; may she who gave you birth rejoice!

PROVERBS 23:24, 25 NIV

STRATEGY

SEVEN

PREPARE YOUR KIDS FOR LIFE

The end goal of parenting is to help our kids spread their own wings and fly on their own. Preparing them for life begins when they are young. Step by step and all along the way, we teach our children life lessons so they can be successful and positive adults.

Increasing Their Social IQ

At one point or another (usually during the middle-school years), most kids have days when they come home and declare, "No one likes me." And we parents begin to worry and fret that our child will grow up to be some sort of social misfit or outcast. We want the best for our kids, and that includes solid, long-lasting friendships. Further-more, we've all known people who perhaps weren't at the top of their class academically, but who went far in life because of their ability to work with people. A high social-intelligence quotient can indeed open many doors for people in work, in relationships, and in a variety of life situations.

Daniel Goleman, author of *Social Intelligence: The New Science of Human Relationships*, says, "Empathy and social skills are the two main ingredients of social intelligence. This includes being able to sense another's feelings and intentions. We're now learning that social intelligence also includes the ability to use our inborn neurological links to others in the best possible way."[14] Although we are born with a certain natural social ability, Goleman says we can improve our social IQ if we try.

So, as we prepare our children for life, we want to help them sharpen their social skills. Below are several basic tips you will want to teach your kids to help increase their social IQ and enable them to interact with people in healthy, positive ways:

Be Aware of Social Cues — Pay attention to people's body language and the tone of their voice.

Live by the Golden Rule — Treat others the way you want to be treated.

Be a Good Listener — Maintain eye contact and truly listen to the person.

Choose to Care about Other People — Take an interest in their interests and needs.

Don't Talk about Yourself Unless Asked — Engage others by getting them to talk about themselves.

Be a Positive Person — People do not gravitate toward continually negative people.

Seek to Grow — Ask for an honest social critique from a close friend or family member. Read a book on social etiquette. Decide to make positive changes in how you interact with people.

Learn from Every Challenge — Don't give up in the face of difficulties. Grow up instead.

Be Confident — Even if you don't feel confident, act confident and the feelings will follow. You will put people at ease when you're confident, but you make others nervous when you're nervous.

Have a Sense |of Humor — Encourage laughter with good, clean humor. Never indulge in humor at the expense of another person. Learn to laugh at yourself when something goes wrong.

Maintain a Variety of Friends — Do not cling to one or two. Instead, broaden your circle of friendship by making new friends while keeping the old ones.

Trust God — Don't depend on people alone. Put your trust in God. You may not understand His ways, but you can trust His love for you.

The best way to help your kids learn these truths is to provide them with opportunities for social interaction especially when they are young. I encourage you to open your home to your kids' friends; let your house be the place where kids want to hang out. Also, look for opportunities to do things with others. Get together with another family after church for lunch or go to the park or the zoo with friends. We can help increase our kids' social skills as we schedule, but not force, times with friends. Open your door and your heart to their friends, and you will teach your kids social skills not only by experience but by your own example.

What Every Child Should Know Before Leaving Home

When my kids were preparing to leave for college, I began to panic: *Have I taught them everything they need to know?* My mind started racing through a list of a million things I should have taught them—things like how to change a tire, when to call a doctor, how to cook rice, how to change the vacuum cleaner bags. You know, all the important things in life. I actually sent them off to college without knowing how to sew a button on a shirt.

But before you nominate me for the Bad Mom Award, I do think there is one essential skill that I did teach my kids, and that skill seems to cover all the bases. What is it? Be a learner.

Now, I'm not just talking about being a learner while in the college classrooms. I mean being a learner in the classroom of life. Most of us will never be rocket scientists, but we can learn the essentials in life if we choose to have a teachable spirit and a can-do attitude. And in case you're worried that you may miss a lesson or two along the way as you prepare your kids for life, let me assure you if you teach them to be good learners, you give them a very valuable lesson for life. So here are a few skills to teach your kids about being a good learner.

Ask Good Questions — When you recognize that you don't know how to do something, you can save yourself a great deal of time and frustration if you will ask the right person a good question. Don't feel bad that you don't know it all, and don't think your question is stupid. Seek out someone who can kindly and wisely help you learn. If someone makes you feel stupid for asking a question, that person has a problem, not you.

Here are a few things to keep in mind when you are seeking help:

- ✒ Ask someone who is wise and trustworthy.
- ✒ Ask the person to teach you the skill, not to do what needs to be done for you.
- ✒ Timing is everything. Don't bother a person who is overloaded with other responsibilities.
- ✒ Don't keep asking the same person.
- ✒ Be sure to check the Internet to see if you can find reliable advice or assistance there.

Learn from Tough Times and Mistakes — Trials in life can often sow seeds of beautiful qualities and strengthen our character. Therefore we do our kids a real disservice by trying to shield and protect them from every hurt and pain. Certainly we don't want to lead them into harm's way, but on the other hand we shouldn't be afraid of life's school of hard knocks. Some of their greatest strengths may develop from their disappointments, mistakes, and rough experiences. In fact, every mistake we make is an opportunity to learn and grow. So teach your kids to look at challenges and mistakes as learning opportunities instead of failures.

Also, teach your kids that we never graduate from the classroom of life. We will be learning and growing until the day we die. When they get discouraged with themselves, remind your kids that no one is perfect and that you, too, are still growing and learning.

Read, Read, Read — A good learner is a reader. We grow as people and become better people by reading good books. So make time each day to read. Besides giving us help for specific areas in life, books can also broaden our perspective on life, help us see the bigger picture, and increase our understanding of human nature. Grow as a person one book at a time.

Finally, consider what Benjamin Barber, a political-science professor at Rutgers University, said about the importance of learning:

> I don't divide the world into the weak and the strong, or the successes and the failures, those who make it or those who don't. I divide the world into learners and nonlearners. There are people who learn, who are open to what happens around them, who listen, who hear the lessons. When they do something stupid, they don't do it again. And when they do something

that works a little bit, they do it even better and harder the next time. The question to ask is not whether you are a success or a failure, but whether you are a learner or a nonlearner.[15]

We may not be experts in every area, but we can find the help and answers we need if we are willing to be teachable and believe we can learn. So if your kids don't know exactly how to clean an oven or change the oil in the car, never fear. If you have taught them to be good learners, then you have given them the biggest benefit of all.

Working Hard or Hardly Working?

Working hard for a living seems to get a bad rap these days. Everywhere we look we find get-rich-quick ideas and opportunities to get something for nothing. This Easy Street mentality implies that work is something to be feared or dreaded. In contrast to these messages from our culture, our kids need to have a healthy, biblical understanding of the value of work; kids need to see work as a blessing, not a curse.

A. W. Tozer reminds us of this truth that work is not a curse:

When God put Adam and Eve in the garden, He did not put them there to sit and look at each other and to hold hands. He said they were to take care of the garden. You remember that—they were given something to do. Some people believe that work is a result of the curse, but that's not true. The idea is abroad that the man who works is a boob, and that work is only for fools—but God made us to work.[16]

And I believe we help our kids learn a valuable life lesson when we encourage them to enjoy work.

After all, our work can bring us joy and satisfaction in life whereas laziness has very few redeeming qualities. King Solomon wrote quite a bit about the lazy man as opposed to the one who works, and he used one of the smallest creatures on earth to make his point. In Proverbs 6:6–11 we read this:

Take a lesson from the ants, you lazybones. Learn from their ways and be wise! Even though they have no prince, governor, or ruler to make them work, they labor hard all summer, gathering food for the winter. But you, lazybones, how long will you sleep? When will you wake up?

I want you to learn this lesson: A little extra sleep, a little more slumber, a little folding of the hands to rest—and poverty will pounce on you like a bandit; scarcity will attack you like an armed robber.

A student once wrote a letter to the famous orator and author Henry Ward Beecher, asking his advice in how to obtain "an easy job." Read Mr. Beecher's answer:

If that's your attitude, you'll never amount to anything. You cannot be an editor or become a lawyer or think of entering the ministry. None of these professions is easy. You will have to forget the fields of merchandizing and shipping, abhor the practice of politics, and forget about the difficult field of medicine. To be a farmer or even a good soldier, you must study and think. My son, you have come into a hard world. I know of only one easy place in it, and that is in the grave.[17]

For our kids, a strong work ethic and an appreciation of the value of work both begin with our own attitude. We can encourage our kids' love for work by letting them know how much we choose to enjoy the work that we do whether it is cleaning around the house, volunteering at school, or working at the office. If our kids hear us whine and complain, they will begin to get the idea that work is drudgery instead of something to be valued. Help your kids understand that they may not be able to choose the perfect job, but they can choose their attitude about any job. There is something good to be discovered about every chore and every job, and they can choose to find it.

Of course your kids will want to find work that fits their interests, gifts, or talents. But to be realistic, we must acknowledge that there are times when we must take the somewhat-mundane jobs in life. These can be opportunities to learn to serve others and to practice the discipline of holding down a job responsibly. So never downplay any job, whether it is a mom raising her kids or an engineer out in the field. Every job has its merit; every job teaches us lessons for life. ✽

*Through your actions, your words, your
behavior, and your love, you can direct your
children toward where you want them to go.*

—

Dr. Phil

CONCLUDING THOUGHTS

Joy in our Job as Moms

It is my sincere desire to help and encourage you to be the best mom you can be. Notice I didn't say I want you to be a supermom. I know you're not perfect; neither am I. But with God's help, you and I can be the kind of loving and encouraging mom we have always wanted to be. Remember, God is able to use our strengths as well as our weaknesses as He helps us raise healthy, well-balanced kids. Where we are weak, He is strong. As we turn to Him, He gives us strength, wisdom, and guidance for each day in our amazing (and slightly stressful) role as mothers. So enjoy these bright ideas, but more importantly enjoy His presence with you as you implement them in your daily life.

Have you never heard or understood?
Don't you know that the LORD is the everlasting
God, the Creator of all the earth? He never grows
faint or weary. No one can measure the depths
of his understanding. He gives power to those
who are tired and worn out; he offers strength
to the weak.

—

Isaiah 40:28, 29

NOTES

1. Edward K. Rowell, ed., *Fresh Illustrations for Preaching and Teaching: From* Leadership Journal(Grand Rapids: Baker, 1997), 148.

2. Roy B. Zuck, ed., *The Speaker's Quote Book* (Grand Rapids: Kregel Academic & Professional, 1997), 291.

3. Amy Steedman, *When They Were Children: Stories of the Childhood of Famous Men and Women* (Edinburgh, England: Ballantyne, Hanson & Co.), 117 "T. Nelson and Sons, 1926"

4. http://casacolumbia.org/absolutenm/articlefiles/380-2005_family_dinners_ii_final.pdf.

5. John Blanchard, ed., *More Gathered Gold* (Hertfordshire, England: Evangelical Press, 1986), 102.

6. Philip Yancey, *The Jesus I Never Knew* (Grand Rapids: Zondervan, 1995), 136–37.

7. William F. Russell, *Classics to Read Aloud to Your Children* (New York: Crown Publishers, 1984), 10.

8. For more information about Sonshine Girls, you can visit Karol's Web site at www.PositiveLifePrinciples.com.

9. Jennifer McKnight-Trontz, *The Good Citizen's Handbook: A Guide to Proper Behavior* (San Francisco: Chronicle Books, 2001), 6.

10. All quotes from Walter B. Knight, ed., *Knight's Master Book of New Illustrations* (Grand Rapids: William B. Eerdmans Publishing, 1956), 27–29.

11. Ibid., 423.

12. C. S. Lewis, *Letter to Malcolm: Chiefly on Prayer* (New York: Harcourt Brace Javanovich, 1964), 28.

13. Glenn Van Ekeren, ed., *Speakers Sourcebook II* (Englewood Cliffs, NJ: Prentice Hall, 1994), 133.

14. Daniel Goleman, "Can You Raise Your Social IQ?" in *Parade* Magazine, Sept. 3, 2006.

15. Van Ekeren, 230–31.

16. Charlie "Tremendous" Jones, ed., *Quotes Are Tremendous* (Mechanicsburg, PA: Executive Books, 1995), 189.

17. Van Ekeren, 395